This Book
Belongs to:

Consultant: Fiona Moss, RE Adviser at RE Today Services
Editor: Cathy Jones
Designer: Chris Fraser
QEB Project Editor: Tasha Percy

Copyright © QEB Publishing, Inc. 2015

First published in the United States by
QEB Publishing, Inc.
3 Wrigley, Suite A
Irvine, CA 92618

www.qed-publishing.co.uk

A CIP record for this book is available from the Library of Congress.

ISBN 978 1 60992 264 1

Printed in China

Jonah and the Big Fish

Written by Katherine Sully
Illustrated by Simona Sanfilippo

QEB

QEB Publishing

Most of the time, Jonah was a good man.

Nineveh

So one day, God asked Jonah to do a job for him.

"Go to the city of Nineveh, and deliver a message for me."

But Jonah didn't want to go to Nineveh.
Instead he ran away.

Jonah found a boat to take him far away from Nineveh.
He hid below deck and fell fast asleep.

As he slept, the wind blew and the waves crashed.

A storm rocked the boat, and still Jonah slept!

The captain of the boat came to wake Jonah.

"How can you sleep in this storm!"
cried the captain.
"Get up and say a prayer!"

The boat rocked this way and that way.
The sailors were all afraid.
"Throw the cargo overboard!"
the captain cried.

But it was no use. The storm grew wilder and wilder. "It's my fault," said Jonah. "I didn't do as God asked me." The sailors were shocked and afraid.

"God is angry with me," said Jonah.
"Throw me overboard and the storm will stop."

Now, the sailors didn't really want to throw
Jonah overboard. They prayed and prayed.
But still the storm rocked the boat.

Finally, they threw Jonah SPLOSH! into the waves.

SPLOSH!

And the storm stopped!

Jonah sank through the water,
deeper
and
deeper.

Jonah began to pray:
"I'm sinking down!
Don't let me drown!"

Then he saw a great big fish swim toward him.
The fish opened its mouth wide, wider—

and swallowed him
in one gulp.

GULP!

Jonah sat inside the fish's belly.
He had plenty of time to think. He had run
away from God and was punished.

He had prayed to God
and was saved. Now Jonah thanked
God, and God forgave him.

After three days, the big fish burped.

Jonah shot out of its mouth and landed on a beach!

This time, Jonah went to the city of Nineveh to deliver God's message.

The people there were wicked. They didn't listen to God either.

For three days Jonah walked
through the city, calling,
"Mend your ways in forty days
or Nineveh will be destroyed!"

When they heard Jonah's message from God,
the people of Nineveh were shocked.

Even the King of
Nineveh was shocked.

They had forgotten that God was watching them.

They were very sorry that they had been bad and decided to be good from then on.

So God forgave them.

Jonah sat on a hill outside Nineveh and
waited for the city to be destroyed.

But it was very hot and
nothing happened.
Jonah became very grumpy.

God said to Jonah, "Why are you grumpy? I forgave you because I love you. I forgave the people of Nineveh because I love them."

And finally, Jonah understood that God's love was big enough for everyone.

Next Steps

Look back through the book to find more to talk about and join in with.

* Copy the actions. Pretend you are in a boat being tossed by the waves. Pretend you are a fish. Make a wave action with your hand and arm.

* Join in with the rhyme. Pause to encourage joining in with "I'm sinking down! Don't let me drown!"

* Count the days. Jonah is inside the big fish for three days. Nineveh has 40 days to mend its ways. Talk about how long three days is and how long 40 days is.

* Name the colors of the fish together, then look back to spot the colors on other pages.

* Find shapes and sizes. Compare the big fish with the other fishes on the page.

* How big is the big fish compared with the boat?

* Listen to the sounds. When you see the word on the page, point and make the sound—Splosh! Gulp!

Now that you've read the story...what do you remember?

* Who was Jonah?
* Why did he run away to sea?
* Where did Jonah end up when he was thrown into the sea?
* How did Jonah get out of the big fish?
* What happened when Jonah got to Nineveh?
* Why did Jonah become grumpy?

What does the story tell us?
If we do the wrong thing, God will show us the right thing to do.